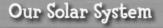
Saturn
The Ringed Planet

By Daisy Allyn

Gareth Stevens
Publishing

Please visit our Web site, www.garethstevens.com. For a free color catalog of all our high-quality books, call toll free 1-800-542-2595 or fax 1-877-542-2596.

Library of Congress Cataloging-in-Publication Data

Allyn, Daisy.
 Saturn : the ringed planet / Daisy Allyn.
    p. cm. — (Our solar system)
 Includes index.
 ISBN 978-1-4339-3840-5 (pbk.)
 ISBN 978-1-4339-3841-2 (6-pack)
 ISBN 978-1-4339-3839-9 (library binding)
 1. Saturn (Planet)—Juvenile literature. I. Title.
 QB671.A44 2011
 523.46—dc22
                                          2010001055

First Edition

Published in 2011 by
Gareth Stevens Publishing
111 East 14th Street, Suite 349
New York, NY 10003

Copyright © 2011 Gareth Stevens Publishing

Designer: Christopher Logan
Editor: Greg Roza

Photo credits: Cover, back cover, pp. 1, 7, 17 (bottom), 19 courtesy NASA/JPL/Space Science Institute; p. 5 Shutterstock.com; p. 9 courtesy NASA, ESA, Martin Kornmesser (ESA/Hubble); p. 11 courtesy NASA, ESA and Erich Karkoschka (University of Arizona); p. 13 © 2002 Calvin J. Hamilton; p. 15 (both) courtesy NASA/JPL/University of Colorado; pp. 17 (top), 21 courtesy NASA/JPL.

Printed in the United States of America

CPSIA compliance information: Batch #CS10GS: For further information contact Gareth Stevens, New York, New York at 1-800-542-2595.

Contents

Boldface words appear in the glossary.

Meet the Ringed Planet

Saturn is the sixth planet from the sun. It is the second-largest planet in our **solar system**. Rings made of ice and dust circle Saturn.

Our Solar System

Neptune

Uranus

Saturn

Jupiter

Mars

Earth

Venus

Mercury

sun

5

On the Move

Saturn **orbits** the sun just like the other planets do. Saturn takes about $29\frac{1}{2}$ years to travel once around the sun!

Saturn

sun

Saturn spins around just like the other planets do. It spins very quickly. Saturn only takes about $10\frac{1}{2}$ hours to spin around once.

9

A Gas Giant

Thick clouds surround Saturn. The clouds are made mostly of a gas called **hydrogen**.

Inside Saturn

Beneath Saturn's clouds, most of the planet is made up of liquid hydrogen and **helium**. Saturn's center, or core, is hot and rocky.

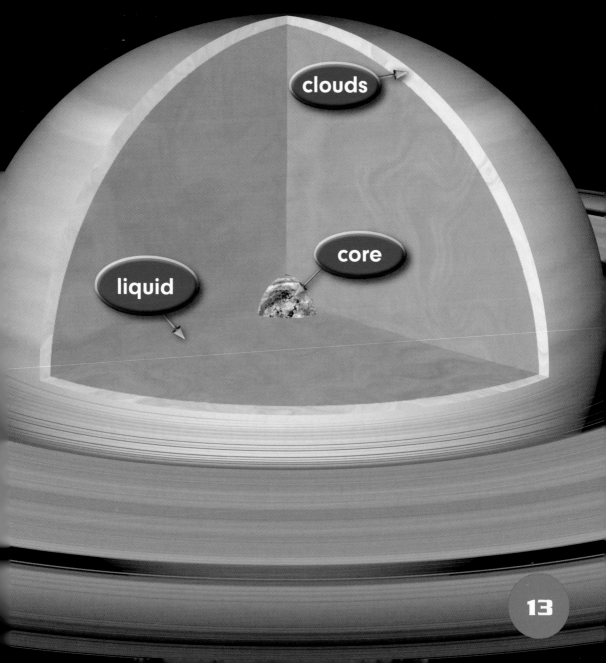

Saturn's Rings

Saturn has rings around it. The rings are made mostly of ice **chunks**. The ice chunks orbit Saturn just like Saturn orbits the sun.

Saturn's rings

ice chunks

The Moons of Saturn

Saturn has more than 60 moons! Some are very big, and some are very small. Saturn's smallest known moon is only about $\frac{1}{3}$ mile ($\frac{1}{2}$ km) wide.

oons

one of Saturn's moons

Saturn's largest moon is Titan. It is the second-largest moon in the solar system. It's bigger than the planet Mercury! Unlike Saturn, Titan is mostly rock and ice.

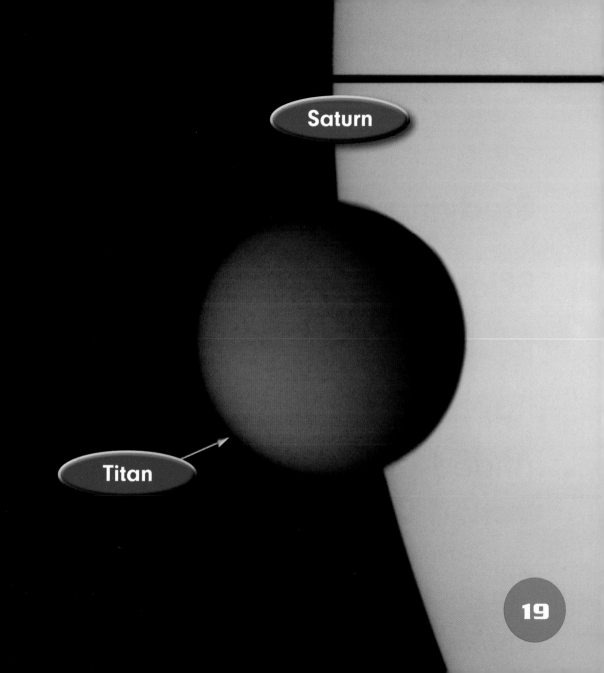

Saturn

Titan

19

Studying Saturn

Scientists have sent **probes** to study Saturn. The probes have told us a lot about the ringed planet.

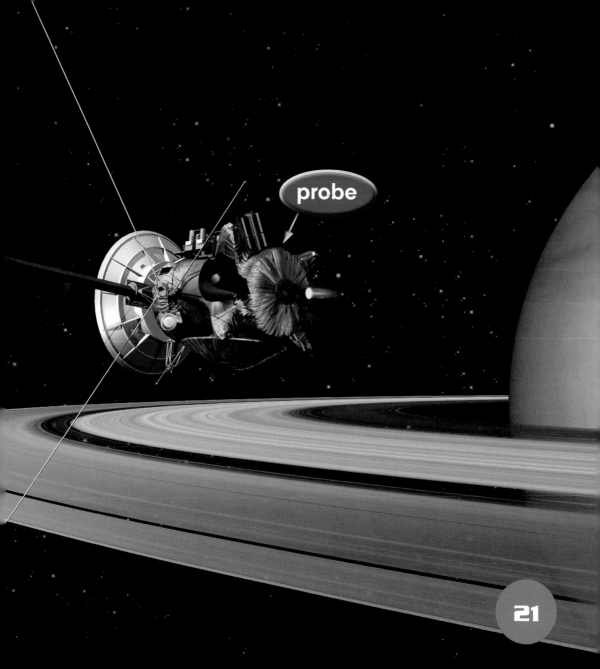

probe

Glossary

chunk: an uneven piece of something

helium: one of the most common gases in the solar system.

hydrogen: a common gas. The most common matter in the solar system.

orbit: to travel in a circle or oval around something

probe: an unmanned spaceship

solar system: the sun and all the space objects that orbit it, including the planets and their moons

For More Information

Books

Taylor-Butler, Christine. *Saturn*. New York, NY: Children's Press, 2008.

Wimmer, Teresa. *Saturn*. Mankato, MN: Creative Education, 2008.

Web Sites

Cassini–Huygens: Kids Space
saturn.jpl.nasa.gov/kids/index.cfm
This NASA web site has information about the mission of the Cassini-Huygens probe sent to study Saturn and its moons.

Saturn
www.kidsastronomy.com/saturn.htm
Learn basic facts about Saturn and its moons.

23

Index

About the Author

Daisy Allyn teaches chemistry and physics at a small high school in western New York. A science teacher by day, Allyn spends many nights with her telescope, exploring the solar system. Her Great Dane, Titan, often joins Allyn on her nightly stargazing missions.